How Bat Learned to Fly

Long ago, the animal people played a ball game.

3

Mouse was not
a good player.

He dropped the ball
when he was running.

4

"Why do you always drop the ball?" cried Coyote.

"He can't hold it," said Raccoon.

"His hands are too small," said Possum.

"Hold it under your arm," said Raccoon.

"No, hold it under your chin, like this," said Possum.

But Mouse could not
hold the ball.

Mouse was sad.
He went away.

Mother Earth saw Mouse.

"Do not be sad, Mouse,"
she said. "When you see
the ball coming, jump up
and catch it with your body."

"I am a good jumper,"
said Mouse. "Thank you,
Mother Earth.
I will try jumping."

15

So, next time Mouse played, he jumped high into the air.

He caught the ball with his body.

17

No one could catch him.

19

"I can fly," said Mouse.
"I can fly."

"Yes," said Mother Earth. "You can fly. You are not Mouse. Now, you are Bat."

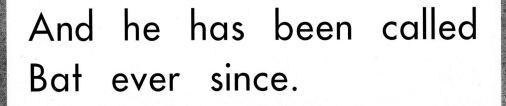

And he has been called
Bat ever since.